THE HORSES OF
Appleby Fair

Heidi M Sands

Old Pond
PUBLISHING LTD

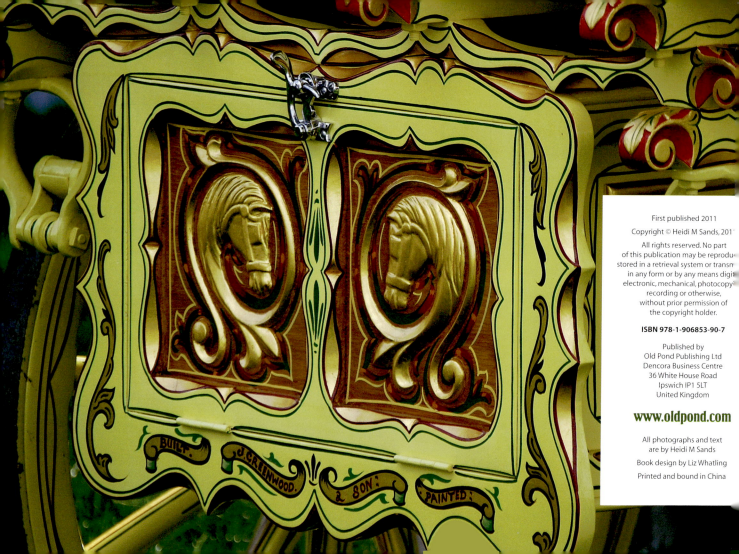

First published 2011

Copyright © Heidi M Sands, 2011

All rights reserved. No part
of this publication may be reprodu
stored in a retrieval system or transm
in any form or by any means digit
electronic, mechanical, photocopy
recording or otherwise,
without prior permission of
the copyright holder.

ISBN 978-1-906853-90-7

Published by
Old Pond Publishing Ltd
Dencora Business Centre
36 White House Road
Ipswich IP1 5LT
United Kingdom

www.oldpond.com

All photographs and text
are by Heidi M Sands

Book design by Liz Whatling

Printed and bound in China

Introduction

Each June the roads that make their way to the English town of Appleby in Cumbria ring out with the footfalls of horses. Along with the trailers that carry some of the lucky equines to this most famous of horse fairs are strings of horse-drawn vehicles, the most recognisable of which are the bow-top caravans. A horse-drawn journey to Appleby is slow and can take several weeks depending on where it began, for travellers and their horses come from all over the UK and Ireland to be at one of the most important gatherings of the year.

The horses of Appleby Horse Fair are diverse, colourful, flamboyant, dependable and tough.

In abundance are the vanners; those who literally pull the 'vans or caravans, the older type of living accommodation, home to travellers before more modern caravans appeared on the scene. Sometimes with Fell or Dales pony blood, these horses are great weight carriers and are often broken for both riding and driving.

These are the true gypsy cobs, standing anywhere between 13.2 and 15 hands high. They carry plenty of feather around their heels and are either piebald (black and white), skewbald (brown and white), or darker solid colours, with tremendous hair in their manes and tails. These are generally understood to be the traditional horses of the gypsy, Romany or travelling people.

Alongside these at Appleby you will also see a lighter, leggier horse used in trotting races. Usually a whole colour, possibly bay or chestnut, this will be a speed merchant harnessed to a light gig – and boy can these trotters go.

Smaller ponies, used for children to ride or to pull a smaller type of trap, are also found at Appleby. Many have Shetland pony as their origin; others may carry some Welsh pony blood. Most are crossbreeds and will be valued for their calm, unflappable natures, vital when they are in close proximity to children.

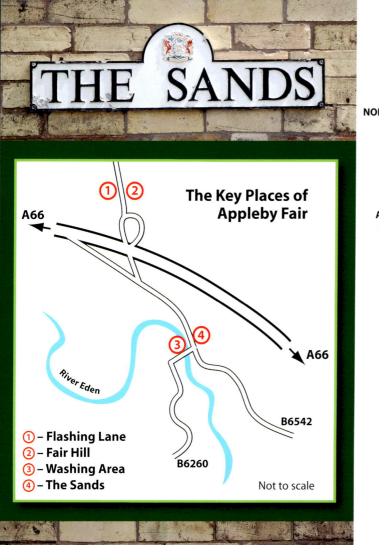

THE SANDS

The Key Places of Appleby Fair

- A66
- River Eden
- ① ②
- ③ ④
- B6542
- B6260

① – **Flashing Lane**
② – **Fair Hill**
③ – **Washing Area**
④ – **The Sands**

Not to scale

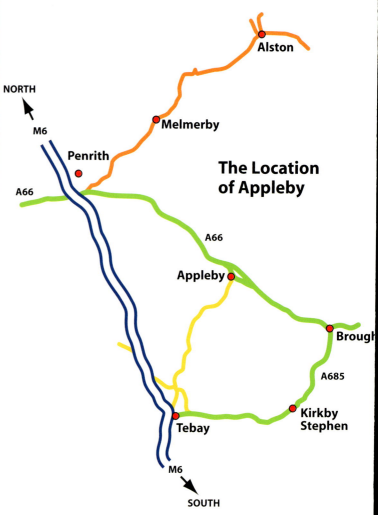

The Location of Appleby

- NORTH
- Alston
- Melmerby
- M6
- Penrith
- A66
- A66
- Appleby
- Brough
- A685
- Tebay
- Kirkby Stephen
- M6
- SOUTH

It is not uncommon to see a mare at Appleby with her youngster at her side, for she is capable of doing a job of work as well as rearing a good foal, provided she is well cared for and adequately fed. The foals or younger horses at Appleby, cute and endearing, come in all shapes and sizes depending on their parentage.

Tradition is all-important to the travelling community and nowhere is this more in evidence than at the area of Appleby known as The Sands. Here the river Eden flows through the centre of the town, and a shallow entry makes the water accessible to horses. Deeper pools in this part of the river are utilised by some of the younger, usually male, horse handlers, encouraging their horses to swim. Crowds gather to watch the spectacle and to see the horses washed, bathed and readied for selling. On occasion horses are turned or become loose here, several banding together to drink, paw the water or move as one, splashing as they go.

Leaving the river, ridden in most cases, the horses head in spectacular fashion uphill, mingling with vehicular traffic, other horses and horse-drawn vehicles until they reach the area known as the flashing lane. Here horses are tied in number, protective rails are provided along what is more usually a vehicle highway but is shut off for the 'flashing' or parading of horses. Speed is an essential and horses are shown or flashed to attract potential buyers.

All manner of animals parade along the well-lined route. Stallions from Ireland hold themselves proud, screaming to attract attention; steady, stately cobs catch the eye of those looking to buy a decent driving horse, and boys and young men race two abreast in lighter gigs along the tarmac surface. Tied horses swing on their tethers to watch or graze quietly on the longer roadside grasses. Some stretch out full length to catch the warmth of the summer sunshine and everywhere people mingle, taking in the spectacle that in one short weekend can see the exchange of thousands of pounds on the slap of a hand.

It is all about the horses at Appleby. Up on Fair Hill the stalls reflect this. Here it is possible to buy all manner of tack and saddlery, crockery decorated with images of horses and in among the glitz and glamour of the younger generation, ponies are tethered

and traps, wagons and flat carts await their owner's return.

The green fields of Appleby's farms are turned into caravan and car parks for the duration with areas set aside for rows of horse-drawn 'vans, highly decorated in traditional style. The horses are never far away, for these are part of the family for travellers. In a quieter area a veterinary surgeon may treat a minor equine ailment. Children groom or tack up their own ponies and, encouraged by their elders, join in the family atmosphere. But this is no Saturday afternoon gymkhana and there are no prizes; this is the biggest horse fair in Europe. With origins that stretch back as far as the 1700s, this is all about the buying and selling of horses.

Once it is all over, the horses are hitched up to their caravans, loaded into their wagons and move on. Some will wend their way to a permanent home; others may spend the remainder of the summer following age-old byways, tethered along other roadsides, or move on to other horse fairs. Wherever they go and whatever they do, a percentage will be back the following year to be part of another Appleby Horse Fair.

Come with me to Appleby Fair and take a look at the horses that make this gathering unique in the horse world.

Arriving at Appleby in traditional style.

Arriving

Travellers converging on Appleby are increasingly encouraged to plan their journeys so as not to arrive too far in advance of the fair itself.

Those with horse-drawn vehicles may well have had a long journey and for these reasons several temporary stopping places and transit sites are set aside to provide parking areas for traditional bow tops, motor vehicles and caravans as well as grazing areas for horses.

One such is at Melmerby where gypsies and travellers are welcome to stop at the village green on both inward and outward journeys to and from Appleby. Here horses graze on long tethers and rest awhile. Colour is provided by the handsomely decorated traditional living wagons and old friends meet up to chat and swap news.

Melmerby is a quiet rural area of Cumbria, where the road leaves the relatively lower ground and climbs up to Alston via Hartside.

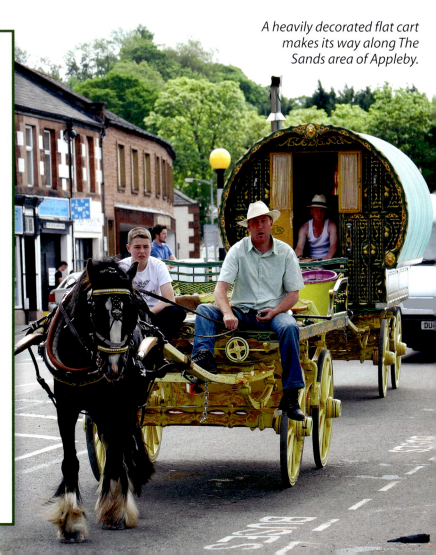

A heavily decorated flat cart makes its way along The Sands area of Appleby.

With harness close by, the living wagon will soon be on the road to Appleby once more.

*Lined up together, these traditional
living wagons make a spectacular sight.*

Time to stop awhile and pass the time of day at Melmerby.

*Pegged out on their own space, the horses seldom come into conflict
with others, preferring instead to watch the comings and goings.*

*Cobs graze
the short
sweet grass.*

Some of these horses are real heavyweights.

Beauty on the green.

NOTICE

No Camping, Bow Tops
Trailers or Vehicles
of any description
allowed in this area

**This area is for
horse grazing only**

Eden
District Council

Restrictions apply.

This black-and-white stallion parades his own area on the green.

Preferring to rest as evening approaches.

All manner of vehicular traffic collects together in an orderly manner at Melmerby.

Under the lilac tree.

Even travellers' horses wear fly fringes to keep the worst of the flies away.

Horses and their transport in close proximity.

Black-and-white cobs predominate.

While some horses graze others indulge in mutual grooming.

You can never have enough grass.

Horses are always interested in what's going on.

Some horses travel to the fair in style.

It can be a long, hard pull uphill for one horse so sometimes a second is drafted in to help.

Spare horses often follow on behind the living wagons.

Trotting on.

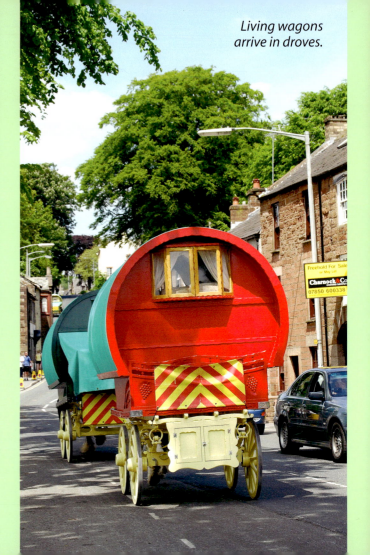

Living wagons arrive in droves.

Horses have right of way in Appleby.

Bow tops crossing the Eden.

Steady does it through Appleby.

No mistaking name or trade.

Flat carts bring the whole family to town.

Simply flying with all four feet off the ground.

Cobs r us – a smart turnout.

Some horses may need a little persuasion.

Washing and The Sands

One of the highlights of the fair is the washing of horses in the river Eden at the area of Appleby known as The Sands. Here a specially constructed ramp makes access in and out of the water easier for man and beast.

All manner of horses are led down Appleby's main street, some singly, others in teams, some with foals at foot. Making their way on to the shingle, they drink in the shallows or venture further out into the river with their handlers. Several deeper pools encourage the horses to swim, and with riders on their backs they forge ahead creating a spectacular sight. Elsewhere horses are scrubbed clean, bathed and given a good washing down – much to the delight of the onlookers.

Now clean and spruced up, bare–chested young men show off the prowess of these horses, trotting along in the shallows before hauling their charges out onto the street once more, to dry off in the summer sun.

This rider holds a branch aloft – trophy or token?

It's easier with two to help wash a horse down.

The face says it all – it can be cold in the water.

Emerging from the water.

Trotting out through the shallows.

Watching from the safety of the furthest bank.

The heavy mob hits town.

A stunning example of a black-and-white cob heads down to the river.

Together in
the river.

The typical bareback position of an Appleby rider.

Sometimes whole strings of horses are brought down into the water.

Washing-up liquid comes into its own here.

Being led towards the washing area.

Heading back uphill to dry off after a swim.

Crowds of spectators.

*Stepping out smartly
after a dip in the water.*

Taking a rest.

Rinsing the horse off is all-important.

Perfect Appleby.

Groups of young men gather at The Sands area to wash and water their horses.

Eye-catching in and out of the water.

Up the ramp to dry off.

Spectators must heed the signs.

The next string of horses arrives to take to the water.

Keeping an eye on proceedings.

Staying close to Mum while she has a drink.

Testing the water.

A stylish pair making for the Eden.

*Heading down
to The Sands.*

*Although riders are
usually young men,
young women can
handle horses too.*

Riding bareback is typical at Appleby.

Flashing the Horses

In layman's terms the flashing of a horse is to show it off. In Appleby's terms it is the opportunity for the owners, riders and showmen to exhibit horses in all their glory and attract attention to their charges with the intention of gaining a sale. In other words, the flashing of a horse at Appleby is the chance to display him or her as you would goods in a shop window.

Horses at Appleby are traditionally flashed on what is known as the flashing lane, but is more usually the Long Marton road, which leads out of town. For the main three days of the fair the road is closed to vehicular traffic, so busy does it become with horses. In reality the road is still used to flash and display horses on other fair days, competing with other road users for space and tarmac. Flashing also takes place in other areas of Appleby – for what showmen, or women, would not take any opportunity to show off their horses' paces!

Trotting out.

Mounted police, here at The Sands, keep an eye on all goings-on.

Tied up and waiting.

A real stunner.

A friendly chat, or a deal about to be done?

Riding into town.

Who will win?

It's a close-run thing with an equally matched pair.

Little and large.

A smart landau-style vehicle.

Taking the whole family for a drive.

It's never too early for a rest.

Steady does it at the approach to the Long Marton road.

Watching what's going on.

The rails along the flashing lane are used for tethering.

Eye-catching and waiting his turn.

A pastoral scene on the flashing lane.

All manner of horses are admired along the flashing lane

DANGER
POLICE WARNING

Racing along.

The whip seller sits out in the sun awaiting trade.

All the way from Ireland to strut his stuff at Appleby.

Pretty in pink.

Bespoke.

A knot in it for luck.

Grazing at the side of the road.

This feathered cob proceeds in a stately manner along the flashing lane.

High-stepping along the lane.

Two-way traffic.

The road can become congested with horses.

Under the living wagon.

Fair Hill and Around

All manner of visitors will stay.

Fair Hill sits just outside Appleby. For most of the year it is agricultural land, but for one week it becomes awash with colour. Here gypsies and travellers park their homes and set up their stalls. All manner of wares including decorated crockery, kettles, stunning dresses, embroidered children's outfits and pram covers sit side by side with horse requisites, tack and driving equipment. Whole families gather together to buy what they need at Appleby.

Between the stalls and in the fields around Fair Hill horses graze or are moved around. Heavily decorated and eye-catching, living wagons, sometimes known as vardos, or bow tops, are parked in groups or ones and twos. Friends and families gather together on Fair Hill to spend time in each other's company and swap news – for this is truly a family affair.

Some horses travel in modern lorries.

Living wagons sit side by side.

Grazing peacefully in spite of all the goings-on.

Following his master.

Hand painted by a craftsman

Traditional handcart.

Shining in
the sun.

Who wouldn't want to buy?

The living wagon or vardo.

Three ages of man.

Golden array.

Horses are everywhere.

Tethered in the sun.

Buying what they need.

So beautiful.

Traditional wares.

Fine art is everywhere.

Even terrets need homes at Appleby

Resting with the others.

More horses than you can imagine.

*Fields awash
with horses.*

Dozing in the sun.

The runaway captured.

Space for them all.

Harness and driving collars await use.

Ponies for purchase.

Harnessing up.

Moving on.

Moving off.

Beautiful turnouts.

It takes skill to drive through here.

Brothers or good friends?

Heidi M Sands

Born and brought up in the north-west of England, Heidi studied art and design at Preston Polytechnic and also at Blackpool and Fylde College. A life-long equestrian and award-winning writer, Heidi has a deep devotion to that part of Cumbria, once Westmorland, known as the Eden valley, from where generations of her own family originated.

Founded in 1998, Suffolk-based Old Pond specialises in books and DVDs for the land-based industries from farm machinery and animal breeds to earthmoving, trucking and forestry.

Free catalogue:
Old Pond Publishing, Dencora Business Centre, 36 White House Road, Ipswich IP1 5LT, United Kingdom

www.oldpond.com

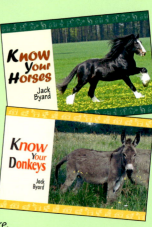